I0118853

Joseph Berry

Songs of the Soul

For use in Sunday evening congregations, revivals, camp-meetings, social

services and young peoples meetings

Joseph Berry

Songs of the Soul
*For use in Sunday evening congregations, revivals, camp-meetings, social services
and young peoples meetings*

ISBN/EAN: 9783337266172

Printed in Europe, USA, Canada, Australia, Japan

Cover: Foto ©Thomas Meinert / pixelio.de

More available books at **www.hansebooks.com**

FOR USE IN

SUNDAY EVENING CONGREGATIONS,

REVIVALS, ...

CAMP-MEETINGS, .

SOCIAL SERVICES, AND

YOUNG PEOPLE'S MEETINGS.

EDITED BY
JOSEPH F. BERRY AND JAMES M. BLACK.

"let all the people sing."

CRANSTON & CURTS,
CINCINNATI, - CHICAGO, - ST. LOUIS.
HUNT & EATON,
NEW YORK, BOSTON, PITTSBURG, SAN FRANCISCO.
1894.

Prefatory Note.

RECIOUS goods are often put up in small packages. The saying is true of this little book. These songs are soulful. They will speak to hearts, and cause hearts to speak. They are songs of Christ and salvation.

SONGS OF THE SOUL is published in response to an urgent demand for a low-priced book especially adapted for congregational singing, revivals, camp-meetings, social services, and young people's devotional meetings. Many of the best standard hymns are associated with the most popular gospel songs of our day. Considering the size and excellence of the book, the price will surprise every one. It is certainly within reach of all.

The editors hope that the little book may help inaugurate a great revival of Christian song in the Churches, and that it may be made a blessing to many thousands of hearts. LET ALL THE PEOPLE SING.

THE EDITORS.

Copyright 1894, by CRANSTON & CURTS.

Copyright, 1894, by Cranston & Curts.

Songs of the Soul.

No. 1. Jesus the Light of the World.

G. D. E. arr.

GEO. D. ELDERKIN, arr.

1. Hark! the her-ald an-gels sing,   Je-sus the Light of the world;
2. Joy - ful, all ye na-tions, rise,   Je-sus the Light of the world;
3. Christ by high - est heav'n adored,   Je-sus the Light of the world;
4. Hail the heav'n-born Prince of peace,   Je-sus the Light of the world;

Glo - ry to the new - born King,   Je-sus the Light of the world.
Join the tri-umphs of the skies,   Je-sus the Light of the world.
Christ, the ev - er - last - ing Lord,   Je-sus the Light of the world.
Hail the Sun of right-eous-ness,   Je-sus the Light of the world.

CHORUS.

We'll walk in the light, beautiful light, Come where the dewdrops of mercy are bright,

Shine all a-round us by day and by night, Je-sus the light of the world.

COPYRIGHT, 1890, BY GEO. D. ELDERKIN.

A

1

No. 2. There's Cleansing in the Precious Blood.

REV. ISAAC NAYLOR.   JAMES M. BLACK.

1. Oh! hasten now to Calv'ry's mountain, There's cleansing in the precious blood;
2. "Come now, togeth-er let us reason," There's cleansing in the precious blood;
3.   Your heart is full of sin and sadness, There's cleansing in the precious blood;
4. At morning, noon and night I'm singing, There's cleansing in the precious blood;

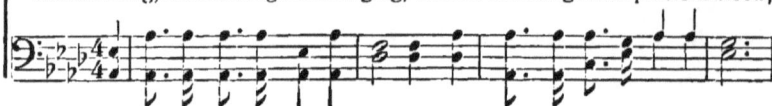

And plunge in-to the flowing fountain, There's cleansing in the precious blood.
Although your sins be red like crimson, There's cleansing in the precious blood.
In Je - sus there is joy and gladness, There's cleansing in the precious blood.
Oh, let us keep the anthem ringing, There's cleansing in the precious blood.

CHORUS.

There's cleansing in the precious blood, Plunge now beneath the crimson flood;

Con-fess-ing all your sins to Je-sus, There's cleansing in the precious blood.

COPYRIGHT, 1894, BY J. M. BLACK.

2

No. 3. Jesus Is Passing By.

E. E. HEWITT.

JNO. R. SWENEY.

1. Come, contrite one, and seek his grace, Je - sus is pass - ing by;
2. Come, hungry one, and tell your need, Je - sus is pass - ing by;
3. Come, wea-ry one, and find sweet rest, Je - sus is pass - ing by;
4. Come, burdened one, bring all your care, Je - sus is pass - ing by;

See in his rec - on - cil - ed face The sunshine of the sky.
The Bread of Life your soul will feed, And ful - ly sat - is - fy.
Come where the longing heart is blessed, And on his bo - som lie.
The love that list - ens to your prayer Will "no good thing" de-ny.

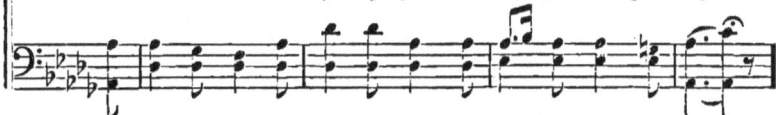

CHORUS.

Pass - ing by, .. Pass - ing by, .. Hasten to meet him on the way,
Passing by, passing by, passing by, passing by,

Jesus is passing by to-day, Pass - - ing by, .. pass - - ing by.
Passing by, passing by, passing by, passing by.

COPYRIGHT, 189 , BY JNO. R. SWENEY.

Wonderful Story of Love.

I. M. D.

Rev. J. M. DRIVER, by per.

Duet.

Full Chorus.

1. Won-der-ful sto-ry of love: Tell it to me a-gain:
2. Won-der-ful sto-ry of love: Tho' you are far a-way:
3. Won-der-ful sto-ry of love: JE-SUS pro-vides a rest:

Won-der-ful sto-ry of love: Wake the im-mor-tal strain!
Won-der-ful sto-ry of love: Still he doth call to-day;
Won-der-ful sto-ry of love: For all the pure and blest:

An-gels with rap-ture announce it, Shepherds with wonder re-ceive it;
Calling from Calvary's mountain, Down from the crys-tal bright fountain,
Rest in those mansions a-bove us, With those who've gone on before us,

Sin-ner, O won't you be-lieve it? Won-der-ful sto-ry of love.
E'en from the dawn of cre-a-tion, Won-der-ful sto-ry of love.
Singing the rap-tur-ous cho-rus, Won-der-ful sto-ry of love.

CHORUS.

Won - der - ful! Won - der - ful!
Won-der-ful story of love: won-der-ful sto-ry of love:

Wonderful Story of Love. Concluded.

Won - der - ful!
Won - der - ful sto - ry of love! Won - der - ful sto - ry of love!

No. 5. Step Out on the Promise.

E. F. MILLER, by per.

1. Oh mourn-er of Zi - on, how bless - ed art thou, For Je - sus is
2. Oh ye that are hun - gry and thirst-y, re - joice! For ye shall be
3. Who sighs for a heart from in - iq - ui - ty free? Oh, poor troub-led
4. The promise do n't save, tho' the promise is true; 'Tis the blood we get

wait - ing to com - fort thee now; Fear not to re - ly on the
filled; do you hear that sweet voice In - vit - ing you now to the
soul! there's a prom - ise for thee; There's rest, wea-ry one, in the
un - der that cleanseth us thro'; It cleans - es me now, hal - le-

word of thy God Step out on the promise,—get un - der the blood.
ban-quet of God? Step out on the promise,—get un-der the blood.
bo - som of God; Step out on the promise,—get un-der the blood.
lu - jah to God! I rest on the promise,—I'm un-der the blood.

COPYRIGHT, 1884, BY E. F. MILLER.

5

No. 6. Oh, The Blood.

Words and Melody furnished by Isaac Naylor.

1. O when shall my soul find her rest, My strugglings and wrestlings be o'er;
2. Now search me and try me, O Lord! Now, Je-sus, give ear to my cry;
3. My i-dols I cast at Thy feet, My all I re-turn Thee who gave;
4. O Sav-ior, I dare to be-lieve! Thy blood for my cleans-ing I see;

My heart by my Sav-ior possessed, By fear-ing and sin-ning no more?
See! help-less I cling to Thy word, My soul to my Sav-ior draws nigh!
This mo-ment the work is com-plete, For Thou art al-might-y to save.
And, ask-ing in faith, I re-ceive Sal-va-tion full, pres-ent, and free!

CHORUS.

Oh, the blood - - - - - - the precious blood - - - - - - Oh, the
Oh, the blood, the precious blood,

blood, it cleans-eth me, - - - - - - - - - Oh, the
Oh, the blood, it cleans-eth me, it cleans-eth me,

blood, - - - the precious blood, - - - - - The blood, it cleans-eth me.
Oh, the blood, the precious blood,

COPYRIGHT, 1894, BY CHAS. H. GABRIEL.

6

No. 7. Where He Leads I'll Follow.

W A. O.

W. A. OGDEN.

1. Sweet are the prom-is-es, Kind is the word, Dear-er far than
2. Sweet is the ten-der love Je-sus hath shown, Sweeter far than
3. List to his lov-ing words, "Come un-to me;" Wea-ry, heav-y

an-y mes-sage man ev-er heard; Pure was the mind of Christ,
an-y love that mortals have known; Kind to the err-ing one,
la-den, there is sweet rest for thee; Trust in his prom-is-es,

Sin-less I see; He the great ex-am-ple is and pattern for me.
Faith-ful is he; He the great ex-am-ple is and pattern for me.
Faith-ful and sure; Lean up-on the Sav-ior and thy soul is se-cure.

CHORUS.

Where he leads I'll fol low,
Where he leads I'll fol-low, Where he leads I'll fol-low,

1.
Fol low all the way,
Follow all the way, yes, follow all the way.

2.
Follow Jesus ev'ry day

COPYRIGHT, 1886, BY W. A. OGDEN.

7

No. 8.   The Call for Reapers.

J. O. Thompson.
Spirited.

J. B. O. Clemm.

1. Far and near the fields are teem - ing With the waves of
2. Send them forth with morn's first beam - ing, Send them in the
3. O thou, whom thy Lord is send - ing, Gath - er now the

rip - ened grain; Far and near their gold is gleam-ing O'er the
noon - tide's glare; When the sun's last rays are gleam-ing Bid them
sheaves of gold, Heavenward then at even - ing wend-ing, Thou shalt

Chorus.

sun - ny slope and plain.
gath - er ev - 'ry - where.   Lord of har - vest, send forth
come with joy un - told.

reap - ers! Hear us, Lord, to thee we cry; Send them now the

sheaves to gath - er, Ere the har - vest time pass by.

BY PER. HUNT & EATON, AGENTS, OWNERS OF COPYRIGHT.

8

No. 9. Leaning on the Everlasting Arms.

Rev. E. A. HOFFMAN.   A. J. SHOWALTER.

1. What a fel-lowship, what a joy divine, Leaning on the ev - er-
2. Oh, how sweet to walk in this pilgrim way, Leaning on the ev - er-
3. What have I to dread, what have I to fear, Leaning on the ev - er-

last - ing arms; What a bless - ed-ness, What a peace is mine,
last - ing arms; Oh, how bright the path grows from day to day,
last - ing arms? I have bless - ed peace with my Lord so near,

REFRAIN.

Lean - ing on the ev - er - last - ing arms. Lean - ing,
Lean - ing on the ev - er - last - ing arms.
Lean - ing on the ev - er - last - ing arms. Lean - ing on Je - sus,

lean - ing, Safe and se-cure from all a - larms;
Lean - ing on Je - sus,

Lean - ing, lean - ing, Leaning on the ev-er-lasting arms.
Leaning on Je-sus, leaning on Je-sus,

BY PER. A. J. SHOWALTER.

9

Sweet Voices.

REV. DWIGHT WILLIAMS.   J. M. BLACK.

1. Hear sweet voic - es from a - bove, Fill thy hands and go with love
2. Cups of wa - ter ye may bear, And bring an-swer to your pray'r;
3. On - ly tell the sto - ry how Je - sus comes to bless you now;

To the wear - y as they wait, So late; In the
Je - sus led the mul - ti - tude With good. How the
What you do for love is best Con - fessed. Go as

name of Christ your King, Go and sweet-ly, sweet-ly sing, Go and
blind with o-pened eyes Looked on Him with glad sur-prise! Love may
Je - sus went to them; You may find perchance a gem, Long to

CHORUS.

wipe their tears a - way, And pray. Hap-py voic - - - - es Ev - 'ry-
fix the eyes long dim On Him.
spar - kle in His sight In light.   Hap-py voic-es

where,   Are like an - - - - - gels in the
Ev - 'ry - where   Are like an - - gels,

COPYRIGHT, 1894, BY J. M. BLACK.

air.
an - gels in the air. 'T was for this that Je - sus came, There is

mu - sic in his name, In the work he call - eth you, Be true.

No. 11.   Rock of Ages.

AUGUSTUS M. TOPLADY, alt.   THOS. HASTINGS.

FINE.

1. Rock of A - ges, cleft for me, Let me hide my - self in thee;
2. Could my tears for - ev - er flow, Could my zeal no lan-guor know,
3. While I draw this fleeting breath, When my eyes shall close in death,

D. C.—Be of sin the dou-ble cure, Save from wrath and make me pure.
In my hand no price I bring; Simply to thy cross I cling.
Rock of A - ges, cleft for me, Let me hide my - self in thee;

D. C.

Let the wa - ter and the blood, From thy wounded side which flowed,
These for sin could not a - tone; Thou must save, and thou a - lone:
When I rise to worlds unknown, And behold thee on thy throne,

11

No. 12. Beneath the Shade of the Cross.

Words and Melody furnished by ISAAC NAYLOR.

1. If you want pardon, and in - fi - nite peace, If you want sighing and
2. If you want Je - sus to reign in your soul, Plunge in the fountain and
3. If you want boldness, take part in the fight; If you want pu - ri - ty,
4. If you want ho - li - ness, cling to the cross, Counting the rich - es of

sor-row to cease, Look up to Je - sus who died on the tree To
you shall be whole, Wash'd in the blood of the cru - ci - fied One, En-
walk in the light; If you want lib - er - ty, shout, and be free, En-
earth as but dross; Down at His feet you'll be wealthy and wise, En-

CHORUS.

pur-chase a full sal - va - tion.
joy-ing a full sal - va - tion.
joy-ing a full sal - va - tion. Liv-ing beneath the shade of the cross,
joy-ing a full sal - va - tion.

Count-ing the jew - els of earth but dross, Cleansed in the blood that

flowed from His side, En - joy - ing a full sal - va - tion.

COPYRIGHT, 1893, BY CHAS. H GABRIEL.

Welcome For Me.

FANNY J. CROSBY.

WM. J. KIRKPATRICK.

1. Like a bird on the deep, far a-way from its nest, I had
2. I am safe in the ark; I have fold-ed my wings On the
3. I am safe in the ark; and I dread not the storm, Tho' a-

wandered, my Sav-ior, from thee; But thy dear lov-ing voice called me
bo-som of mer-cy di-vine; I am filled with the light of thy
round me the sur-ges may roll; I will look to the skies, where the

home to thy breast, And I knew there was welcome for me.
pres-ence so bright, And the joy that will ev-er be mine.
day nev-er dies, I will sing of the joy in my soul.

CHORUS.

Welcome for me, Sav-ior from thee; A smile and a welcome for me:

Now, like a dove, I rest in thy love, And find a sweet refuge in thee.
in thee.

COPYRIGHT, 1885, BY W. J. KIRKPATRICK.

13

No. 14. The Joyful Tidings.

"Preach the gospel to every creature."—Mark 16: 15.

F. M. D.   FRANK M. DAVIS.

1. Spread the joy-ful ti-dings Of redeeming love, How the Lord of glo - ry
2. Spread the joy-ful ti-dings O - ver land and sea, Of the grace that saves men,
3. Spread the joy-ful ti-dings, Death has lost its sting, And the grave its vic-t'ry,

Left his home a - bove; Tell the precious sto - ry, How for man he
Sets the bondmen free; Nations now in darkness, Lost in er-ror's
Let the ti-dings ring; Je- sus, King tri - umphant, High the an-them

died, Of the heal - ing foun-tain Flow-ing from his side.
night, Pit - y then their blindness, Send them joy - ful light.
raise, Till all earth and hea - ven Swell the song of praise.

CHORUS.

Spread the ti - - - - dings, joy-ful sound, ... To the
Spread the joyful ti-dings, Spread the joyful ti-dings,

BY PERMISSION.

The Joyful Tidings. Concluded.

earth's . . . remotest bound; How the Lord . . . . of glo-ry
earth's remotest bound, earth's remotest bound, Lord of glory died,

died, How for sin-ful man was cru - ci - fied, cru - ci-fied.
Lord of glo - ry died,

No. 15. Mourn for the Thousands Slain.

UNKNOWN. LOWELL MASON.

1. Mourn for the thou-sands slain, The youth-ful and the strong;
2. Mourn for the ru - ined soul— E - ter - nal life and light
3. Mourn for the lost,—but call, Call to the strong, the free;
4. Mourn for the lost,—but pray, Pray to our God a - bove,

Mourn for the wine-cup's fear-ful reign, And the de - lud - ed throng.
Lost by the fie - ry, maddening bowl, And turned to hopeless night.
Rouse them to shun that dreadful fall, And to the ref - uge flee.
To break the fell de - stroy-er's sway, And show his sav - ing love.

No. 16. The Blood of Jesus.

2d and 3d stanzas by C. D. E. Arr. by C. D. EMERSON.

1. We'll shout and sing, make heaven ring with prais - es to our King,
2. In cheer - full lays our voi - ces raise to him our songs of praise;
3. His name so sweet, his love complete we own, and kiss his feet;

Who bled and died, was cru - ci - fied that he might par - don bring;
We loud pro - claim his bless - ed name, and won - ders of his ways,
To pu - ri - fy and sanc - ti - fy, his prom - i - ses are meet!

His blood can save a soul, can cleanse and make it whole—
While this, the sto - ry sweet, we joy - ful - ly re - peat—
All glo - ry to his name with rapt - ure we pro - claim—

The blood of Je - sus cleans-eth white as snow, white as snow!

CHORUS.

The blood of Jesus cleanseth white as snow, white as snow, The blood of Jesus

WORDS AND ARRANGEMENT, COPYRIGHT, 1884, BY CHAS. H. GABRIEL.

The Blood of Jesus. Concluded.

cleanseth white as snow, white as snow! I bless the hap-py day when he
washed my sins away, The blood of Jesus cleanseth white as snow, white as snow.

No. 17. There is a Fountain.

W. COWPER.

LOWELL MASON.

1. There is a foun-tain filled with blood, Drawn from Im-man-uel's veins,
2. The dy-ing thief re-joiced to see That foun-tain in his day;
3. Dear dy-ing Lamb! thy precious blood Shall nev-er lose its power,
4. E'er since, by faith, I saw the stream Thy flow-ing wounds sup-ply,
5. Then in a no-bler, sweet-er song, I'll sing thy power to save,

FINE.

And sin-ners plunged beneath that flood, Lose all their guilt-y stains.
And there may I, though vile as he, Wash all my sins a-way.
Till all the ran-somed Church of God Be saved to sin no more.
Re-deem-ing love has been my theme, And shall be till I die.
When this poor lisping, stammering tongue Lies si-lent in the grave.

D. S.

Lose all their guilt-y stains, - - - - Lose all their guilt-y stains.
Wash all my sins a-way, - - - - Wash all my sins a-way.
Be saved to sin no more, - - - - Be saved to sin no more.
And shall be till I die, - - - - And shall be till I die.
Lies si-lent in the grave, - - - - Lies si-lent in the grave.

B

17

No. 18.　　　He Saves Me.

REV. G. MURRAY KLEPFER.　　　　　　　　　　　　　J. M. BLACK.

1. A con-trite sin-ner at the mer-cy seat, He saves me to-day:
2. I trust the mer-its of the Cru-ci-fied, He saves me to-day;
3. To doubt and fear I will no long-er cling, He saves me to-day;
4. He fills me dai-ly with his Spir-it's pow'r, He saves me to-day,

I lay my bur-den at the Sav-ior's feet, He saves me to-day.
I feel the cleansing of the blood ap-plied, He saves me to-day.
The Ho-ly Spir-it doth as-sur-ance bring, He saves me to-day.
His grace is vic-t'ry in the try-ing hour, He saves me to-day.

REFRAIN.

He saves me, He saves me O glo-ry to his precious name!
He saves me now, He saves me now,

I lay my bur-den at the Sav-ior's feet, He saves me to-day.
I feel the cleansing of the blood ap-plied, He saves me to-day.
The Ho-ly Spir-it doth as-sur-ance bring, He saves me to-day.
His grace is vic-t'ry in the try-ing hour, He saves me to-day.

COPYRIGHT, 1894, BY J. M. BLACK

No. 19. Sitting at the Feet of Jesus.

1. { Sit-ting at the feet of Je - sus, Oh, what words I hear him say!
   { Happy place! so near, so precious! May it find me there each   day!
2. { Sit - ting at the feet of Je - sus, Where can mortal be more blest?
   { There I lay my sins and sor-rows, And, when weary, find sweet   rest:
3. { Bless me, Oh my Savior, bless me, As I sit low at thy feet;
   { Oh, look down in love up - on me, Let me see thy face so   sweet.

{ Sit-ting at the feet of Je - sus, I would look upon the past :
{ For his love has been so gracious, It has won my heart at   last.
{ Sit-ting at the feet of Je - sus, There I love to weep and pray,
{ While I from his full-ness gather Grace and com-fort ev-'ry   day.
{ Give me, Lord, the mind of Jesus, Make me ho - ly as he is;
{ May I prove I 've been with Jesus, Who is all my right-cous-   ness.

No. 20. I 'll Live for Him.

C. R. DUNBAR.

1. My life, my love I give to thee, Thou Lamb of God, who died for me;
2. I now be-lieve thou dost receive, For thou hast died that I might live;
3. Oh Thou who died on Cal-va-ry, To save my soul and make me free,

CHO. *I 'll live for him who died for me, How hap-py then my life shall be!*

D. C.

Oh may I ev - er faith - ful be, My Sav - ior and my God!
And now henceforth I 'll trust in thee, My Sav - ior and my God!
I con - se - crate my life to thee, My Sav - ior and my God!

I 'll live for him who died for me, My Sav - ior and my God!

BY PERMISSION OF R. E. HUDSON, OWNER OF COPYRIGHT.

No. 21. Not Ashamed of Jesus.

JOSEPH GRIGG.   CHAS. H. GABRIEL.

Duet for Tenor and Contralto.

1. Je - sus, and shall . . . it ev-er be, ... A mortal man . . . .
2. Ashamed of Je - - sus! sooner far . . . . Let evening blush . . .
3. Ashamed of Je - - sus! just as soon. . . . Let midnight be . . . .
4. Ashamed of Je - - sus! yes, I may, . . . When I've no guilt . . .

ashamed of thee? . . Ashamed of thee, . . whom angels praise, . . .
to own her star; . . . He sheds the beams . . of light di - vine . . . .
ashamed of noon; . . 'T is midnight with . . my soul till he, ...
to wash a - way; . . No tear to wipe, . . no good to crave, . . .

CHORUS.

Whose glo-ries shine thro' endless days.   Ashamed of Je - sus I
O'er this be-night-ed soul of mine.
Bright Morning Star, bids darkness flee.
No fears to quell, no soul to save.   Ashamed of Je-sus I

nev - er, I nev - er will be, ... For my dear
nev - er, I nev - er will be, I nev - er will be,   For

COPYRIGHT, 1894, BY CHAS. H. GABRIEL.

Not Ashamed of Jesus. Concluded.

Sav - ior is not ashamed of me; . . . . . .
my dear Sav - ior is not ashamed, is not ashamed of me;

No, when I blush . . . . . be this my shame, ...
No, when I blush, be this my shame,

That I no more re - vere his name.
That I no more re - vere his name.

No. 22. Cross and Crown.

THOMAS SHEPHERD.   GEO. N. ALLEN.

1. Must Je - sus bear the cross a - lone, And all the world go free?
2. How hap - py are the saints a - bove, Who once went sorrowing here!
3. The con - se - crat - ed cross I 'll bear, Till death shall set me free;

No, there 's a cross for ev - 'ry one, And there 's a cross for me.
But now they taste un - min - gled love, And joy with - out a tear.
And then go home my crown to wear, For there 's a crown for me.

21

No. 23. Sunshine of Love.

Rev. Richard H. Gilbert.   J. M. Black.

1. In this world, where shadows Dark and drear a-bound, Where the tears of
2. Souls in darkness grop-ing, Seek-ing for the way, Lead-ing up to
3. Soon will end the work-time, And the pain and strife, Then we'll rest to-

sor - row Plen - ti - ful are found, Let us prove our un - ion
glo - ry, Realm of end - less day; Com-fort, cheer and help them,
geth - er Blest with peace and life; With our lov - ing Sav - ior

With the Christ a - bove, By the joy of show-ing Bright sun-shine of love.
Doubt and fear re - move, Making plain the pathway With sun-shine of love.
Now enthroned a - bove, Basking then for- ev - er In sun-shine of love.

CHORUS.

1

Sun - shine, sun-shine, com-ing from a - bove, Keep it beaming ev-er,
Sunshine, blessed,

2

Bright sunshine of love, Keep it beaming ev-er, Bright sun-shine of love.

COPYRIGHT 1884, BY J. M. BLACK.

No. 24. He Saves Me To-Day.

JOHN CENNICK. Music and Chorus by DR. S. B. JACKSON.

1. Je-sus, my all, to heav'n is gone, He whom I fixed my hopes up-on;
2. The way the ho-ly prophets went, The road that leads from banishment,
3. Lo! glad I come, and thou, blest Lamb, Shalt take me to thee, as I am;
4. Then will I tell to sin-ners round, What a dear Sav-ior I have found;

His track I see, and I'll pur-sue The nar-row way, till him I view.
The King's highway of ho-li-ness, I'll go, for all his paths are peace.
Nothing but sin have I to give; Nothing but love shall I re-ceive.
I'll point to thy redeeming blood, And say, "Be-hold the way to God."

CHORUS.

I can, I will, I do be-lieve in Je-sus, And I know he

saves me to-day! · I'm free! I'm free! Oh,
Hal-le-lu-jah, I am free!

glo-ry, hal-le-lu-jah! He has washed my sins all a-way!

COPYRIGHT, 1884, BY CHAS. H. GABRIEL.

23

No. 25.

Hide Thou Me.

FANNY J. CROSBY.

REV. ROBERT LOWRY.

1. In thy cleft, Oh Rock of A - ges, Hide thou me; When the
2. From the snare of sin - ful pleas-ure, Hide thou me; Thou, my
3. In the lone - ly night of sor - row, Hide thou me; Till in

fit - ful tem - pest ra - ges, Hide thou me; Where no
soul's e - ter - nal treas - ure, Hide thou me; When the
glo - ry dawns the mor - row, Hide thou me; In the

mor - tal arm can sev - er From my heart thy love for -
world its power is wield - ing, And my heart is al - most
sight of Jor - dan's bil - low, Let thy bo - som be my

ev - er, Hide me, Oh thou Rock of A - ges, Safe in thee.
yielding, Hide me, Oh thou Rock of A - ges, Safe in thee.
pil - low; Hide me, Oh thou Rock of A - ges, Safe in thee.

COPYRIGHT, 1880, BY BIGLOW & MAIN. USED BY PER.

No. 26. Love Divine.

CHAS. WESLEY.   JOHN ZUNDEL.

1. Love di - vine, all love ex - cell-ing, Joy of heav'n to earth come down!
2. Breathe, O breathe thy lov - ing Spir - it In - to ev - 'ry troubled breast!
3. Come, al-might-y to de-liv - er, Let us all thy life re - ceive;
4. Fin - ish, then, thy new cre - a - tion; Pure and spotless let us be;

Fix in us thy hum-ble dwelling; All thy faith - ful mer - cies crown.
Let us all in thee in - her - it, Let us find that sec-ond rest.
Sud-den - ly re - turn, and nev-er, Nev - er more thy temples leave;
Let us see thy great sal - va-tion Per - fect - ly re-stored in thee;

Je-sus, thou art all com-pas-sion, Pure, un-bounded love thou art;
Take a - way our bent to sin-ning; Al-pha and O - me-ga be;
Thee we would be always blessing, Serve thee as thy hosts a - bove,
Changed from glo-ry in - to glo-ry, Till in heav'n we take our place,

Vis - it us with thy sal - va - tion; En-ter ev - 'ry trembling heart.
End of faith as its be-gin - ning, Set our hearts at lib - er - ty.
Pray, and praise thee without ceasing, Glo - ry in thy per-fect love.
Till we cast our crowns before thee, Lost in won-der, love, and praise.

25

Lead Me, Savior.

F. M. D.   FRANK M. DAVIS.

1. Sav - ior, lead me, lest I stray (lest I stray), Gen - tly
2. Thou the ref - uge of my soul (of my soul), When life's
3. Sav - ior, lead me, till at last (till at last), When the

1. Sav - ior, lead me, lest I stray, Gen-

lead me all the way (all the way); I am safe when by thy
storm-y bil - lows roll (bil-lows roll), I am safe when thou art
storm of life is past (life is past), I shall reach the land of

tly lead me all the way; I am

side (by thy side), I would in thy love a - bide (love a-bide).
nigh (thou art nigh), On thy mer - cy I re - ly (I re - ly).
day (land of day), Where all tears are wiped a - way (wiped a-way).

safe when by thy side, I would . . . in Thy love a-bide.

CHORUS.

Lead me, lead me, Sav - ior, lead me, lest I stray; . .
Sav - ior, lead me, lest I stray, lest I stray;

BY PERMISSION.

Lead Me, Savior. Concluded.

Rit - e - dim.

Gen - tly down the stream of time,   Lead me, Sav-ior, all the way.
stream of time,   all the way.

No. 28.   Thou Thinkest, Lord, of Me.

E. D. MUND.   E. S. LORENZ.

1. A - mid the tri - als which I meet, A - mid the thorns that pierce my feet,
2. The cares of life come thronging fast, Up - on my soul their shadows cast;
3. Let shadows come, let shad-ows go, Let life be bright or dark with woe,

Fine.

One thought re - mains su - preme-ly sweet, Thou thinkest, Lord, of me!
Their gloom re - minds my heart at last, Thou thinkest, Lord, of me!
I am con - tent, for this I know, Thou thinkest, Lord, of me!

D. S. What need I fear since Thou art near, And thinkest, Lord, of me.

CHORUS.   D. S.

Thou think-est, Lord, of me,   Thou thinkest, Lord, of me.
of me,   of me.

27

No. 29. Wonderful Army of God.

W. A. S.

W. A. SPENCER, D. D.

1. There's a won - der - ful arm - y now marching, But its war - fare is
2. Floating out o'er this wonder - ful arm - y Is the ban - ner of
3. There's a place in this wonder - ful arm - y For the loy - al, true-
4. All the arm - ies of e - vil must per - ish, But the glo - ri - ous
5. Then all hail to the conquering Chieftain, Who is vic - tor o'er

not one of blood; For by mer - cy and love are the conquests Of the
in - finite love, While the songs of earth's conquering legions Ech-o
hearted and brave, Who will fol - low the blessed Re-deemer, Follow
promise is given, That our arm - y, in youth ev - er - lasting, Shall as-
death and the grave; Swift to rescue the world's darkest province Marches

Chorus.

won - der-ful arm-y of God. Who will march in this wonderful
back from the armies a - bove.
Je - sus, the mighty to save.
sem - ble un - broken in heaven.
Je - sus, the mighty to save.

arm - y, With the ban - ner of Jesus un - furled? Who will march in this

wonderful arm - y, Marching with Je - sus to conquer the world?

COPYRIGHT, 1894, BY W. A. SPENCER.

Blessed Assurance.

FANNY CROSBY.

MRS. JOS. F. KNAPP.

1. Blessed as-sur-ance, Je-sus is mine! Oh, what a fore-taste of
2. Perfect sub-mis-sion, per-fect de-light, Vis-ions of rap-ture burst
3. Perfect sub-mis-sion, all is at rest, I in my Sav-ior am

glo-ry di-vine! Heir of salvation, purchased of God, Born of his
on my sight; Angels descending, bring from above Echoes of
happy and blest; Watching and waiting, looking above, Filled with his

CHORUS.

Spir - it, washed in his blood. This is my sto - ry, this is my
mer - cy, whisp-ers of love.
good-ness, lost in his love.

song, Praising my Sav-ior all the day long; This is my sto - ry,

this is my song, Praising the Sav - ior all the day long.

BY PERMISSION.

My Jesus, I Love Thee.

A. J. GORDON.

1. My Je - sus, I love thee, I know thou art mine;
2. I love thee, be - cause thou hast first lov - ed me,
3. I'll love thee in life, I will love thee in death,
4. In man - sions of glo - ry and end - less de - light

For thee all the fol - - lies of sin I re - sign;
And pur - chased my par - - don on Cal - va - ry's tree;
And praise thee as long as thou lend - est me breath;
I'll ev - er a - dore thee in heav - en so bright;

My gra - cious Re - deem - er, my Sav - ior art thou,
I love thee for wear - ing the thorns on thy brow;
And say when the death - dew lies cold on my brow,
I'll sing with the glit - ter - ing crown on my brow,

If ev - er I loved thee, my Je - sus, 'tis now.

BY PER.

No. 32.   The Cross.

DR. BONAR.   J. R. DUNHAM.

1. The cross it stand-eth fast, Hal-le-lu-jah! hal-le-lu-jah!
2. It is the old cross still, Hal-le-lu-jah! hal-le-lu-jah!
3. 'Twas here the debt was paid, Hal-le-lu-jah! hal-le-lu-jah!

De-fy-ing ev-'ry blast, Hal-le-lu-jah for the cross! The
Its triumphs let us tell, Hal-le-lu-jah for the cross! The
Our sins on Je-sus laid, Hal-le-lu-jah for the cross! So

winds of hell have blown, The world its hate hath shown, Yet 'tis not over-thrown,
grace of God here shown, Thro' Christ, the blessed Son, Who did for sin a-tone,
'round the cross we sing Of Christ, our of-fer-ing,— Of Christ, our liv-ing King,

CHORUS.

Hal-le-lu-jah for the cross! Hal-le-lu-jah! halle-lu-jah! It ne'er shall suffer

loss, Hal-le-lu-jah! hal-le-lu-jah! Hal-le-lu-jah for the cross!

COPYRIGHT, 1898, BY CHAS. H. GABRIEL.

No. 33. We'll Never Say Good=bye.

GEO. C. HUGG.

GEO. C. HUGG.

1. In the morn of morns when we all meet there, In the home far a-
2. Nev-er sad-ness there, neither grief nor tear, In that beau-ti-ful
3. With our kindred dear, in that home of love, While the a-ges e-

bove the sky, We'll re-call the scenes we have left be-hind, But we
home on high! But they swell the song, happy ransomed throng, And they
ter-nal fly, We will meet, and sing, at the Savior's feet, But we

CHORUS.

nev-er will say "good-bye." In the dawn - ing of the
In the dawn-ing clear of the

morn - ing, In that home far a-bove the sky; Hap-py
morn-ing fair,

meet - ing, hap-py greet - ing, When we nev-er say "good-bye."
meeting there, happy greeting there,

COPYRIGHT, 1895, BY GEO. C. HUGG.

32

No. 34.   Sunshine in the Soul.

E. E. HEWITT.   JNO. R. SWENEY.

1. There's sunshine in my soul to-day, More glo-ri-ous and bright
2. There's mu-sic in my soul to-day, A car-ol to my King,
3. There's springtime in my soul to-day, For when the Lord is near,
4. There's gladness in my soul to-day, And hope, and praise, and love,

Than glows in an-y earth-ly sky, For Je-sus is my light.
And Je-sus, list-en-ing, can hear The songs I can-not sing.
The dove of peace sings in my heart, The flow'rs of grace ap-pear.
For blessings which he gives me now, For joys "laid up" a-bove.

REFRAIN.

Oh, there's sun - - - - shine, Bless-ed sun - - - shine,
sun-shine in the soul,   sun-shine in the soul,

While the peace-ful, hap-py mo-ments roll;   When
hap-py moments roll,

Je-sus shows his smiling face There is sun-shine in the soul.

COPYRIGHT, 1887, BY JNO. R. SWENEY.

33

C

No. 35.   The Best Friend is Jesus.

P. B.

Duet. *Sop. (or Ten.) & Alto.*

P. Bilhorn. By per.

1. Oh the best friend to have is Je - sus, When the cares of life up-
2. What a friend I have found in Je - sus! Peace and comfort to my
3. Tho' I pass thro' the night of sor - row, And the chil-ly waves of
4. When at last to our home we gath - er, With the loved ones who have

on you roll; He will heal the wounded heart, He will
soul he brings; Lean-ing on his might-y arm, I will
Jor - dan roll, Nev - er need I shrink or fear, For my
gone be - fore, We will sing up - on the shore, Prais-ing

strength and grace im-part; Oh the best friend to have is Je - sus.
fear no ill or harm; Oh the best friend to have is Je - sus.
Sav - ior is so near; Oh the best friend to have is Je - sus.
him for ev - er-more; Oh the best friend to have is Je - sus.

Chorus.—*Spirited.*

The best friend to have is Je - - - sus, The best friend to have is
Je-sus ev-ery day,

34

The Best Friend is Jesus. Concluded.

Je - - - - sus, He will help you when you fall, He will
Je - sus all the way,

hear you when you call; Oh the best friend to have is Je - sus.

No. 36.   Happy Day.

DODDRIDGE.   RIMBAULT.

1. { Oh hap-py day, that fixed my choice On thee, my Savior and my God! }
   { Well may this glowing heart re-joice, And tell its raptures all a-broad. }
2. { Oh hap-py bond, that seals my vows To him who mer - its all my love! }
   { Let cheerful anthems fill his house, While to that sacred shrine I move. }
3. { 'T is done, the great transaction's done; I am my Lord's, and he is mine; }
   { He drew me, and I followed on, Charmed to confess the voice di-vine. }

FINE.

Hap-py day, hap-py day, When Je-sus washed my sins a - way;
D. S.—Hap-py day, hap-py day, When Je-sus washed my sins a - way.

D. S.

He taught me how to watch and pray, And live re - joic - ing ev - ery day:

Scatter Sunshine.

LANTA WILSON SMITH.   E. O. EXCELL.

1. In a world where sorrow Ev - er will be known, Where are found the
2. Slightest actions oft - en Meet the sorest needs, For the world wants
3. When the days are gloomy, Sing some happy song, Meet the world's re-

need - y, And the sad and lone; How much joy and com - fort
dai - ly, Lit - tle kind - ly deeds; Oh, what care and sor - row
pin - ing With a cour - age strong; Go with faith un-daunt-ed,

You can all be-stow, If you scatter sunshine Ev'rywhere you go.
You may help remove, With your songs and courage, Sympathy and love.
Thro' the ills of life, Scatter smiles and sunshine O'er its toil and strife.

CHORUS.

Scat - ter sun-shine all along your way, Cheer and bless and
Scat-ter smiles and

bright - en Ev-'ry passing day, Ev-'ry pass-ing day.

COPYRIGHT, 1898, BY E. O. EXCELL.

At the Cross.

ISAAC WATTS.   R. E. HUDSON.

1. A - las! and did my Sav - ior bleed, And did my Sovereign die?
2. Was it for crimes that I have done, He groaned upon the tree?
3. But drops of grief can ne'er re - pay The debt of love I owe;

Would he de-vote that sa - cred head For such a worm as I?
A - maz - ing pit - y, grace unknown, And love beyond de - gree!
Here, Lord, I give my-self a - way, 'Tis all that I can do!

CHORUS.

At the cross, at the cross, where I first saw the light, And the

bur-den of my heart rolled away —
rolled a-way,   It was there by faith

I received my sight, And now I am hap-py all the day.

COPYRIGHT, 1885, BY R. E. HUDSON. BY PER.

No. 39. Look and Live.

W. A. O.   W. A. OGDEN.

1. I've a mes-sage from the Lord, Hal-le-lu-jah! The
2. I've a mes-sage full of Love, Hal-le-lu-jah! A
3. Life is of-fered un-to thee, Hal-le-lu-jah! E-
4. I will tell you how I came; Hal-le-lu-jah! To

mes-sage un-to you I'll give, 'Tis re-cord-ed in his word,
mes-sage, oh! my friend, for you, 'Tis a message from a-bove,
ter-nal life thy soul shall have, If you'll on-ly look to him,
Je-sus, when he made me whole; 'Twas be-liev-ing on his name,

Hal-le-lu-jah! It is on-ly that you "look and live."
Hal-le-lu-jah! Je-sus said it; and I know 'tis true.
Hal-le-lu-jah! Look to Je-sus, who a-lone can save.
Hal le-lu-jah! I trust-ed and he saved my soul.

CHORUS.

"Look and live," . . . . . my broth-er, live,
"Look and live," my broth-er, live, "Look and live."

COPYRIGHT. 1887, BY E. O. EXCELL.

Look and Live. Concluded.

Look to Je - sus now and live, 'Tis re - cord - ed in his word,

Hal - le - lu - jah! It is on - ly that you "look and live."

No. 40.   I Stretch My Hands to Thee.

CHARLES WESLEY.

1. Fa - ther, I stretch my hands to thee, No oth - er help I know;
2. What did thine on - ly Son en - dure, Be - fore I drew my breath;
3. O Je - sus, could I this be - lieve, I now should feel thy power;
4. Au - thor of faith, to thee I lift My wea - ry, long - ing eyes;

CHO. *I do be - lieve, I now be - lieve, That Je - sus died for me,*

If thou withdraw thy-self from me, Ah, whither shall I go?
What pain, what la - bor to se - cure My soul from end-less death!
And all my wants thou wouldst re - lieve In this ac - cept - ed hour.
O let me now re - ceive that gift! My soul with-out it dies.

And thro' his blood, his pre-cious blood, I shall from sin be free.

No. 41.   There 's a Wideness.

F. W. FABER.   LIZZIE S. TOURJEE.

1. There 's a wide-ness in God's mer-cy, Like the wideness of the sea;
2. There is wel-come for the sin-ner, And more grac-es for the good;
3. For the love of God is broad-er Than the measure of man's mind;
4. If our love were but more sim-ple, We should take him at his word;

There 's a kind-ness in his jus-tice, Which is more than lib-er-ty.
There is mer-cy with the Sav-ior; There is heal-ing in his blood.
And the heart of the E-ter-nal Is most won-der-ful-ly kind.
And our lives would be all sun-shine In the sweetness of our Lord.

No. 42.   Come Unto Me.

1. Come un-to me when shadows darkly gath-er, When the sad heart is
2. Large are the mansions in thy Father's dwell-ing, Glad are the homes that
3. There, like an E-den blos-som-ing in glad-ness, Bloom the fair flow'rs the

D. S. Come un-to me, and
Soft are the tones which
Come un-to me, and

Fine.   **D. S.**

wea-ry and dis-tressed, Seeking for com-fort from your heav'nly Father.
sor-rows nev-er dim; Sweet are the harps in ho-ly mu-sic swelling.
earth too rude-ly pressed; Come un-to me, all ye who droop in sad-ness,

I will give you rest.
raise the heav'nly hymn.
I will give you rest.

No. 43.   Tell the Story of His Love.

Rev. G. Murry Klepfer.

J. M. Black.

1. Tell the wonderful sto - ry of Je - sus; How from glory to earth he came;
2. Would you lighten the hearts that are heavy? Drive the clouds from the darkened skies?
3. There is full-ness of joy in his presence, There is peace for the reconciled,

How he suffered and died to redeem us; How he lives ev-ermore the same.
Tell the story of grace all-sufficient, And the strength which his love supplies.
Un - to those who believe he is precious, Ev-er near to the trusting child.

Chorus.

Tell the sto - - ry of his love, . . . Spread the
Tell the sto - ry . . . of Je - sus' love,

ti - dings far and near. . . Tell the sto - - - ry
far and near. . . Tell the sto - ry

of his love, . . Tell it out that the world may hear.
of Je - sus' love,

COPYRIGHT 1894, BY J. M. BLACK.

No. 44. It was Spoken for the Master.

LIZZIE EDWARDS.   WM. J. KIRKPATRICK.

1. It was spok-en for the Mas-ter, Oh, how lov-ing-ly it fell!
2. Oh, we know not when we scat-ter, Where the precious seed will fall,
3. When our bus-y toil is o-ver, From the vineyard when we go,

It was ut-tered in a whis-per, Who had breathed it none could tell.
But we work and trust in Je-sus, For he watcheth o-ver all.
We shall find a store of blessings That on earth we could not know.

It was spok-en for the Mas-ter, On-ly just a lit-tle word,
We may sow be-side the wa-ters Of af-flic-tion, it may be,
We shall won-der at the brightness Of the crowns we then shall wear,

But the chords that long had slumbered, In a grief-worn heart were stirred.
But the fruits of earn-est la-bor At the reap-ing we shall see.
But the Lord him-self will tell us Why he placed the jew-els there.

REFRAIN.

Gentle words of patient kindness, Tho' unheed-ed oft they seem,

COPYRIGHT, 1887, BY WM. J. KIRKPATRICK.

It Was Spoken. Concluded.

To the fold of grace may gather Souls of which we lit-tle dream.

No. 45. Hark, the Voice of Jesus Calling.

DANIEL MARCH.   SPANISH MELODY.

1. Hark, the voice of Je-sus call-ing, "Who will go and work to-day?
2. Let none hear you id-ly say-ing, "There is noth-ing I can do,"

Fields are white and harvests wait-ing, Who will bear the sheaves a-way?"
While the souls of men are dy-ing, And the Mas-ter calls for you;

Loud and long the Mas-ter call-eth, Rich re-ward he offers free;
Take the task he gives you glad-ly; Let his work your pleasure be;

Who will an-swer, gladly say-ing, "Here am I, send me, send me?"
Answer quick-ly when he call-eth, "Here am I, send me, send me."

43

No. 46. Stand Up for Jesus.

GEORGE DUFFIELD, JR.

GEORGE JAMES WEBB.

1. Stand up, stand up for Je-sus, Ye soldiers of the cross; Lift high his roy-al
2. Stand up, stand up for Je-sus, Stand in his strength alone; The arm of flesh will
3. Stand up, stand up for Je-sus, The strife will not be long; This day the noise of

ban - ner, It must not suf - fer loss. From vic-t'ry un - to vic- t'ry His
fail you; Ye dare not trust your own: Put on the gos - pel ar-mor, Each
bat - tle, The next the vic-tor's song: To him that o - ver - com-eth, A

ar-my shall he lead, Till ev -'ry foe is vanquished, And Christ is Lord indeed.
piece put on with pray'r; Where duty calls, or dan-ger, Be nev- er wanting there.
crown of life shall be; He with the King of glo - ry Shall reign e - ter- nal- ly.

No. 47. A Charge to Keep.

CHARLES WESLEY.

LOWELL MASON.

1. A charge to keep I have, A God to glo - ri - fy; A
2. To serve the pres - ent age, My call - ing to ful - fill, — O
3. Help me to watch and pray, And on thy - self re - ly, As-

nev - er - dy - ing soul to save, And fit it for the sky.
may it all my pow'rs en - gage, To do my Mas - ter's will.
sured, if I my trust be - tray, I shall for - ev - er die.

44

No. 48. Salvation is Free.

Good as Solo and Chorus.

HARRIET E. JONES.   FRED. A. FILLMORE.

1. I am so glad that sal-va-tion is free, That Je-sus will par-
2. I am so glad that our Sav-ior is King, And needs not the rich-
3. I am so glad that a sin-ner may live, And share in the rich-

don a sin-ner like me; He asks not for sil-ver, he
es the wealth-y would bring; His treas-ures are end-less, his
es this Mon-arch can give; Through a-ges e-ter-nal his

asks not for gold, The poor-est may en-ter the good Shepherd's fold.
rich-es un-told, The poor-est may share in the wealth of his fold.
beau-ty be-hold, And dwell ev-er-more in the cit-y of gold.

CHORUS.

Sal-va-tion is free for you and for me, The Master has rich-es un-told;

Sal-va-tion is free for you and for me; The poorest may en-ter the fold.

COPYRIGHT, 1890, BY FILLMORE BROS.

45

No. 49. Be Not Afraid.

REV. ALFRED J. HOUGH.   CHAS. H. GABRIEL.

1. Come weal, come woe where'er we go, God is not far a - way;
2. Tho' clouds may veil the stars that sail O'er boundless seas of space,
3. Thro' changing years, in joy and tears, The changeless One a - bides,

He holds the storm-y winds that blow, And molds the golden day.
And lights a - long all shores may fail, God will not hide his face;
And safe the soul from doubts and fears That in his bos-om hides.

The dark - est night to him is light, And thro' the shine or shade
But sweet - ly whispers while his hands Up-on his own are laid,—
On nois - y street, in still re-treat, Thro' vales of deepest shade,

He speaks in tones of ten - der might, "My child, be not a - fraid."
"Lo! at thy side thy Father stands, My child, be not a - fraid."
That voice is heard with accents sweet, "My child, be not a - fraid."

COPYRIGHT, 1898, GEO. F. ROSCHE, OWNER OF COPYRIGHT. BY PER.

Be Not Afraid. Concluded.

Be not a - fraid, . . Be not a - fraid, . .
Child, be not, be not a-fraid, Child, be not, be not a-fraid,

The dark - est night to him is light, And thro' the shine or shade,

Be not a - fraid, . . Be not a - fraid, . .
Child, be not, be not a - fraid, Child, be not, be not a-fraid.

He speaks in tones of ten-der might, "My child, be not a - fraid."

No. 50. **Gloria Patri.**

Glory be to the Father, and to the Son,' And to the Ho - ly Ghost,
As it was in the beginning, is now, and ev-er shall be: World without end. A - men.

No. 51.   Just as I Am.

CHARLOTTE ELLIOTT.   WM. B. BRADBURY.

1. Just as I am, with-out one plea, But that thy blood was shed for me,
2. Just as I am, and wait-ing not To rid my soul of one dark blot,
3. Just as I am, tho' tossed about, With many a con-flict, many a doubt,
4. Just as I am, poor, wretched, blind, Sight, riches, healing of the mind,
5. Just as I am, thou wilt receive, Wilt welcome, pardon, cleanse, relieve;

And that thou bidd'st me come to thee,   O Lamb of God, I come, I come!
To thee, whose blood can cleanse each spot, O Lamb of God, I come, I come!
Fight-ings and fears with-in, with-out, O Lamb of God, I come, I come!
Yea, all I need in thee to find,   O Lamb of God, I come, I come!
Be - cause thy prom - ise I be - lieve, O Lamb of God, I come, I come!

No. 52.   Oh For a Thousand Tongues to Sing.

C. WESLEY.   CARL GOTTHELF GLASER.

1. Oh for a thousand tongues, to sing My great Re-deem-er's praise,
2. My gracious Mas-ter and my God, As - sist me to pro - claim,
3. Je-sus! the name that charms our fears, That bids our sor - rows cease;
4. He breaks the power of can-celed sin, He sets the prison-er free;

The glo - ries of my God and King, The tri-umphs of his grace!
To spread through all the earth abroad The hon - ors of thy name.
'Tis mu - sic in the sin-ner's ears, 'Tis life, and health, and peace.
His blood can make the foulest clean; His blood a-vailed for me.

48

No. 53. Scattering Precious Seed.

W. A. OGDEN.

GEO. C. HUGG.

1. Scat-ter-ing precious seed by the way-side, Scat-ter-ing
2. Scat-ter-ing pre-cious seed for the grow-ing, Scat-ter-ing
3. Scat-ter-ing pre-cious seed, doubting nev-er, Scat-ter-ing

pre-cious seed by the hill-side; Scat-ter-ing pre-cious seed
pre-cious seed, free-ly sow-ing; Scat-ter-ing pre-cious seed,
pre-cious seed, trust-ing ev-er; Sow-ing the word with pray'r

o'er the field wide, Scat-ter-ing pre-cious seed by the way.
trusting, know-ing, Sure-ly the Lord will send it the rain.
and en-deav-or, Trust-ing the Lord for growth and for yield.

CHORUS.

Sow - ing in the morn - ing, Sow - ing at the
Sow - ing in the eve - ning,
Sowing the precious seed, Sowing the precious seed, Sowing the seed at noontide,

pp

noon - tide; Sow-ing the precious seed by the way. . . .
Sowing the precious seed; by the way.

BY PER. OF GEO. C. HUGG, OWNER OF COPYRIGHT.

49

No. 54. When the Roll is Called Up Yonder.

E. M. J.　　　　　　　　　　　　　　　　　　　J. M. BLACK.

1. When the trumpet of the Lord shall sound, and time shall be no
2. On that bright and cloudless morning when the dead in Christ shall
3. Let us la - bor for the Mas-ter from the dawn till set-ting

more, And the morning breaks, e - ter - nal, bright and fair; When the
rise, And the glo - ry of his res - ur-rec-tion share; When his
sun, Let us talk of all his wondrous love and care, Then when

saved of earth shall gath - er o - ver on the oth - er shore, And the
chos - en ones shall gath - er to their home beyond the skies, And the
all of life is o - ver and our work on earth is done, And the

CHORUS.

roll is called up yonder, I'll be there. When the roll . . . is
roll is called up yonder, I'll be there.
roll is called up yonder, I'll be there.　　　　When the roll is

called up yon - - - - der, When the roll . . . . is called up
called up yonder, I'll be there, When the roll is called up

COPYRIGHT, 1893, BY CHAS. H. GABRIEL.

50

When the Roll is Called Up Yonder. Concluded.

yon - - - - der, When the roll . . . . is called up
yon - der, I'll be there, When the roll is called up

yon - der, When the roll is called up yon - der, I'll be there.

No. 55. Have Mercy.

1. A - las! and did my Sav - ior bleed, And did my Sovereign die?
2. Was it for crimes that I had done He groaned up - on the tree?
3. Well might the sun in dark - ness hide, And shut his glo - ries in,
4. Thus might I hide my blush-ing face, While His dear cross ap-pears;
5. But drops of grief can ne'er re - pay The debt of love I owe;

Would he de - vote that sa - cred head For such a worm as I?
A - maz - ing pit - y, grace unknown, And love be-yond de - gree!
When Christ, the mighty Mak - er, died For man, the creature's sin.
Dis - solve my heart in thank - ful - ness, And melt mine eyes to tears.
Here, Lord, I give my - self a - way; 'Tis all that I can do.

CHORUS.

Oh Lord, have mer - cy, Oh Lord, have mer - cy,

Oh Lord, have mer - cy, have mer - cy on me.

51

No. 56. There shall be Showers of Blessing.

Ezek. 34: 26.

EL. NATHAN.

JAMES McGRANAHAN.

1. "There shall be show-ers of bless-ing:" This is the promise of love;
2. "There shall be show-ers of bless-ing"— Precious re - viv - ing a - gain;
3. "There shall be show-ers of bless-ing:" Send them up - on us, O Lord;
4. "There shall be show-ers of bless-ing:" Oh that to - day they might fall,

There shall be sea-sons re-fresh-ing, Sent from the Savior a - bove.
O - ver the hills and the val - leys, Sound of abundance of rain.
Grant to us now a re-fresh-ing; Come, and now honor thy word.
Now as to God we're con-fess-ing, Now as on Je - sus we call!

CHORUS.

Show- - - - ers of bless-ing,

Showers, showers of bless-ing, Showers of bless-ing we need;

Mercy-drops round us are fall - ing, But for the showers we plead.

COPYRIGHT, 1883, BY JAMES McGRANAHAN. USED BY PER.

No. 57. My Faith Looks Up to Thee.

RAY PALMER.   L. MASON.

1. My faith looks up to thee, Thou Lamb of Cal-va-ry, Savior divine! Now hear me
2. May thy rich grace im-part Strength to my faint-ing heart, My zeal inspire! As thou hast
3. While life's dark maze I tread, And griefs a-round me spread, Be thou my guide; Bid dark-ness
4. When ends life's transient dream, When death's cold, sul-len stream Shall o'er me roll, Blest Savior,

while I pray; Take all my guilt a-way ; Oh, let me from this day Be wholly thine!
died for me, Oh, may my love to thee Pure, warm, and changeless be—A liv - ing fire!
turn to day, Wipe sorrow's tears a-way, Nor let me ev - er stray From thee a - side.
then, in love, Fear and distrust remove; Oh, bear me safe above—A ransomed soul.

No. 58. Am I a Soldier.

ISAAC WATTS.   THOS. A. ARNE.

1. Am I a sol - dier of the cross, A foll - 'wer of the Lamb,
2. Must I be car - ried to the skies On flow-'ry beds of ease,
3. Are there no foes for me to face? Must I not stem the flood?
4. Sure I must fight, if I would reign ; Increase my cour - age, Lord ;

And shall I fear to own his cause, Or blush to speak his name?
While oth - ers fought to win the prize, And sailed thro' blood - y seas?
Is this vile world a friend to grace, To help me on to God?
I'll bear the toil, en - dure the pain, Sup-port - ed by thy word.

53

No. 59.   Victory Through Grace.

S. MARTIN.

JNO. R. SWENEY.

1. Conquering now and still to conquer, Rideth a King in his might,
2. Conquering now and still to conquer, Who is this won-der-ful King?
3. Conquering now and still to conquer, Je-sus, thou Rul-er of all,

Leading the host of all the faith-ful In - to the midst of the fight;
Whence all the ar-mies which he lead-eth, While of his glo - ry they sing?
Thrones and their scepters all shall per-ish, Crowns and their splendor shall fall,

See them with cour-age ad - vanc-ing, Clad in their brilliant ar - ray,
He is our Lord and Re-deem-er, Sav - ior and Mon-arch di - vine,
Yet shall the ar- mies thou lead-est, Faith-ful and true to the last,

Shouting the name of their Lead-er, Hear them ex - ult - ing - ly say:
They are the stars that for - ev - er Bright in his kingdom will shine.
Find in thy mansions e - ter-nal Rest, when their warfare is past.

COPYRIGHT, 1890, BY JNO. R. SWENEY. USED BY PER. OF J. J. HOOD.

Victory Through Grace. Concluded.

CHORUS.

Not to the strong is the bat-tle, Not to the swift is the race,

Yet to the true and the faithful, Vict'ry is promised thro' grace.

No. 60.   The Way of the Cross.

Arr.

1. I can hear my Savior call-ing, I can hear my Sav-ior call-ing,
2. I'll go with him thro' the gar-den, I'll go with him thro' the gar-den,
3. I'll go with him thro' the judgment, I'll go with him thro' the judgment,
4. He will give me grace and glo-ry, He will give me grace and glo-ry,

D. C. Where he leads me I will fol-low, Where he leads me I will fol-low,

Ad. lib.   D. C.

I can hear my Sav-ior call-ing, "Take thy cross, and follow, fol-low me."
I'll go with him thro' the garden, I'll go with him, with him all the way.
I'll go with him thro' the judgment, I'll go with him, with him all the way.
He will give me grace and glo-ry, And go with me, with me all the way.

Where he leads me I will fol-low, I'll go with him, with him all the way.

55

No. 61. Hail, Thou Whose Sin-atoning Blood.

REV. EARL CRANSTON, D. D.

JOHN HATTON.

1. Hail, thou whose sin - a - ton - ing blood Was typed in
2. Hail, thou whose day on Abra - ham shone, Old Is - rael's
3. Hail, Cal-vary's Lamb, whose conq - 'ring might Led God - hood
4. Hail, Son of Ma - ry, Son of God, Im - man - u -

A - bel's sac - ri - fice; Whom No - ah preached be -
Hope and Proph - ets' theme; The Head and Heir of
cap - tive down to death; Made Jo - seph's tomb a
el, In - car - nate Word, Mes - si - ah, Christ! The

fore the flood, Whose bow of prom - ise guards our skies.
Da - vid's throne, Of a - ges the in - car - nate dream.
throne of light, And filled the grave with quenchless breath.
skies ap - plaud, While na - tions crown thee King and Lord.

No. 62. From all that Dwell.

1 From all that dwell below the skies,
Let the Creator's praise arise ;
Let the Redeemer's name be sung,
Through every land, by every tongue.

2 Eternal are thy mercies, Lord ;
Eternal truth attends thy word :
Thy praise shall sound from shore to shore,
Till suns shall rise and set no more.

3 Your lofty themes, ye mortals, bring;
In songs of praise divinely sing;
The great salvation loud proclaim,
And shout for joy the Savior's name.

4 In every land begin the song;
To every land the strains belong:
In cheerful sounds all voices raise,
And fill the world with loudest praise.

ISAAC WATTS.

No. 63. Jesus Shall Reign.

1 Jesus shall reign where'er the sun
Does his successive journeys run ;
His kingdom spread from shore to shore,
Till moons shall wax and wane no more.

2 From north to south the princes meet,
To pay their homage at his feet ;
While western empires own their Lord,
And savage tribes attend his word.

3 To him shall endless prayer be made,
And endless praises crown his head ;
His name like sweet perfume shall rise
With every morning sacrifice.

4 People and realms of every tongue
Dwell on his love with sweetest song,
And infant voices shall proclaim
Their early blessings on his name.

ISAAC WATTS.

No. 64.   Coronation.

Rev. E. PERRONET.   O. HOLDEN.

1. All hail the pow'r of Je - sus' name! Let an - gels prostrate fall;
2. Let ev - 'ry kin-dred, ev - 'ry tribe, On this ter - res - trial ball,
3. O that with yon - der sa - cred throng We at his feet may fall!

Bring forth the roy - al di - a - dem, And crown him Lord of all.
To him all maj - es - ty ascribe, And crown him Lord of all.
We'll join the ev - er - last-ing song, And crown him Lord of all.

Bring forth the roy - al di - a - dem, And crown him Lord of all.
To him all maj - es - ty ascribe, And crown him Lord of all.
We'll join the ev - er - last-ing song, And crown him Lord of all.

No. 65.   Take my Life and Let it Be.

FRANCES R. HAVERGAL.   C. H. A. MALAN.

1. Take my life and let it be Con-se-cra-ted, Lord, to thee; Take my hands and
2. Take my feet and let them be Swift and beautiful for thee; Take my voice and
3. Take my lips and let them be Filled with messages from thee; Take my silver
4. Take my moments and my days, Let them flow in endless praise; Take my intel-
5. Take my will and make it thine, It shall be no longer mine; Take my heart, it
6. Take my love, my God, I pour At thy feet its treasure-store; Take myself, and

let them move At the impulse of thy love. At the im-pulse of thy love.
let me sing Always—only—for my King. Al-ways—on-ly —for my King.
and my gold, Not a mite would I withhold. Not a mite would I withhold.
lect and use Ev'ry pow'r as thou shalt choose. Ev'ry pow'r as thou shalt choose.
is thine own, It shall be thy roy-al throne. It shall be thy roy-al throne.
I will be Ev-er—on-ly—all for thee. Ev - er—on - ly—all for thee.

57

Go Forth, Ye Heralds.

1. Go forth, ye heralds, in my name, Sweetly the gos-pel trumpet sound;
2. The joyful news to all im-part, And teach them where salvation lies;
3. Freely from me ye have received, Free-ly, in love, to others give;

The glorious ju-bi-lee proclaim, Where'er the human race is found.
With care bind up the broken heart, And wipe the tears from weeping eyes.
Thus shall your doctrines be believed, And, by your la-bors, sin-ners live.

No. 67. Sun of My Soul.

1. Sun of my soul, thou Savior dear, It is not night if thou be near;
2. When the soft dews of kindly sleep My wea-ry eye-lids gently steep;
3. Abide with me from morn till eve, For without thee I cannot live;
4. If some poor wandering child of thine Have spurned, to-day, the voice divine,

O may no earth-born cloud arise To hide thee from thy servant's eyes!
Be my last tho't, how sweet to rest For-ev-er on my Savior's breast.
Abide with me when night is nigh, For without thee I dare not die.
Now, Lord, the gracious work begin; Let him no more lie down in sin.

5 Watch by the sick; enrich the poor,
With blessings from thy boundless store;
Be every mourner's sleep to-night,
Like infant's slumbers, pure and light.

6 Come near and bless us when we wake,
Ere thro' the world our way we take;
Till, in the ocean of thy love,
We lose ourselves in heaven above.

Come, Holy Spirit.

ISAAC WATTS. WILLIAM TANSUR.

1. Come, Ho - ly Spir - it, heav'n- ly Dove, With all thy quicken-ing powers;
2. Look how we grov - el here be- low, Fond of these earth-ly toys;
3. In vain we tune our form - al songs, In vain we strive to rise;
4. Fa - ther, and shall we ev - er live At this poor dy - ing rate,
5. Come, Ho - ly Spir - it, heav'n- ly Dove, With all thy quicken-ing powers;

Kin - dle a flame of sa - cred love In these cold hearts of ours.
Our souls, how heav - i - ly they go, To reach e - ter-nal joys.
Ho - san-nas lan - guish on our tongues, And our de - vo - tion dies.
Our love so faint, so cold to thee, And thine to us so great?
Come, shed a - broad a Sav - ior's love, And that shall kin-dle ours.

No. 69. Spirit Divine.

1 Spirit Divine, attend our prayer,
  And make our hearts thy home;
Descend with all thy gracious power:
  Come, Holy Spirit, come!

2 Come as the light: to us reveal
  Our sinfulness and woe;
And lead us in those paths of life
  Where all the righteous go.

3 Come as the fire, and purge our hearts,
  Like sacrificial flame:
Let our whole soul an offering be
  To our Redeemer's name.

4 Spirit Divine, attend our prayer,
  And make our hearts thy home;
Descend with all thy gracious power:
  Come, Holy Spirit, come!

ANDREW REED.

No. 70. Come, Holy Ghost.

1 Come, Holy Ghost, our hearts inspire:
  Let us thine influence prove;
Source of the old prophetic fire,
  Fountain of life and love.

2 Come, Holy Ghost, for moved by thee,
  The prophets wrote and spoke,
Unlock the truth, thyself the key;
  Unseal the sacred book.

3 Expand thy wings, celestial Dove,
  Brood o'er our nature's night;
On our disordered spirits move,
  And let there now be light.

4 God, through himself, we then shall know,
  If thou within us shine;
And sound, with all thy saints below,
  The depths of love divine.

CHARLES WESLEY.

No. 71. **Turn to the Lord.**

JOSEPH HART.

ANON.
Fine.

1. { Come, ye sin-ners, poor and need-y, Weak and wounded, sick and sore; }
   { Je - sus read - y stands to save you, Full of pit - y, love, and pow'r. }
D. C. Glo - ry, hon - or, and sal - va - tion, Christ, the Lord, has come to reign.

CHORUS.

D. C.

Turn to the Lord and seek sal - va-tion, Sound the praise of his dear name;

2 Now, ye needy, come and welcome,
  God's free bounty glorify ;
  True belief and true repentance,
  Every grace that brings you nigh.

3 Let not conscience make you linger,
  Nor of fitness fondly dream ;

All the fitness he requireth,
Is to feel your need of him.

4 Come, ye weary, heavy-laden,
  Bruised and mangled by the fall,
  If you tarry till you 're better,
  You will never come at all.

No. 72. **Depth of Mercy.**

CHARLES WESLEY.

J. STEVENSON.

1. { Depth of mer - cy! can there be Mer - cy still re - served for me? }
   { Can my God his wrath for - bear, Me, the chief of sin - ners, spare? }

REFRAIN. Faster.

Smoothly.

Repeat *pp*

{ God is love, I know, I feel, }
{ Je - sus weeps and loves me still; } Je - sus weeps, he weeps and loves me still.

2 I have long withstood his grace;
  Long provoked him to his face ;
  Would not hearken to his calls ;
  Grieved him by a thousand falls.

3 Now incline me to repent ;
  Let me now my sins lament ;
  Now my foul revolt deplore,
  Weep, believe, and sin no more.

66

No. 73. Arise, my Soul.

CHARLES WESLEY.   LEWIS EDSON.

1. A - rise, my soul, a - rise; Shake off thy guilty fears; The bleeding Sacri-
2. He ev - er lives a - bove, For me to in - ter-cede; His all - re-deem-ing
3. Five bleeding wounds he bears, Received on Cal-va-ry; They pour effectual
4. My God is rec - onciled; His pardoning voice I hear: He owns me for his

fice In my be - half appears: Be-fore the throne my Surety stands, Be-
love, His precious blood, to plead; His blood atoned for all our race, His
prayers, They strongly plead for me: "Forgive him, Oh forgive," they cry, "For-
child; I can no long - er fear: With con-fi-dence I now draw nigh, With

fore the throne my Surety stands, My name is written on his hands.
blood atoned for all our race, And sprinkles now the throne of grace.
give him, Oh for - give," they cry, "Nor let that ransomed sin - ner die."
con - fi - dence I now draw nigh, And, "Father, Ab-ba, Fath - er," cry.

No. 74. • Jesus, Lover of my Soul.

CHARLES WESLEY.   SIMEON BUTLER MARSH.
FINE.

1. { Je - sus, Lov - er of my soul, Let me to thy bo - som fly, }
   { While the nearer wa - ters roll, While the tempest still is high. }
D. C.—Safe in-to the ha - ven guide; Oh, re-ceive my soul at last.

D. C.

{ Hide me, Oh my Sav - ior, hide, }
{ Till the storm of life is past; }

2 Other refuge have I none;
   Hangs my helpless soul on thee:
Leave, O leave me not alone,
   Still support and comfort me.
All my trust on thee is stayed,
   All my help from thee I bring;
Cover my defenseless head
   With the shadow of thy wing.

3 Plenteous grace with thee is found —
   Grace to cover all my sin;
Let the healing streams abound;
   Make and keep me pure within.

Thou of life the fountain art,
   Freely let me take of thee;
Spring thou up within my heart,
   Rise to all eternity.

61

No. 75.   Come, Ye Disconsolate.

THOS. MOORE, alt.   SAMUEL WEBBE.

1. Come, ye dis-con-so-late, wher-e'er ye lan-guish; Come to the
2. Joy of the des-o-late, light of the stray-ing, Hope of the
3. Here see the bread of life; see wa-ters flow-ing Forth from the

mer-cy-seat, fer-vent-ly kneel; Here bring your wound-ed hearts,
pen-i-tent, fade-less and pure, Here speaks the Com-fort-er,
throne of God, pure from a-bove; Come to the feast of love;

here tell your an-guish; Earth has no sor-row that heav'n can-not heal.
ten-der-ly say-ing, "Earth has no sor-row that heav'n can-not cure."
come, ev-er know-ing, Earth has no sor-row but heav'n can re-move.

No. 76.   Glorying in the Cross.   •

ISAAC WATTS.   ISAAC BAKER WOODBURY.

1. When I sur-vey the wondrous cross On which the Prince of glo-ry died,
2. For-bid it, Lord, that I should boast, Save in the death of Christ, my God;
3. See, from his head, his hands, his feet, Sorrow and love flow mingled down:
4. Were the whole realm of na-ture mine, That were a pres-ent far too small;

My rich-est gain I count but loss, And pour con-tempt on all my pride.
All the vain things that charm me most, I sac-ri-fice them to his blood.
Did e'er such love and sor-row meet, Or thorns com-pose so rich a crown?
Love so a-maz-ing, so di-vine, Demands my soul, my life, my all.

No. 77.   Joy to the World.

I. WATTS.   HANDEL.

1. Joy to the world! the Lord is come; Let earth re-ceive her King; Let
2. Joy to the world! the Sav-ior reigns; Let men their songs employ; While
3. No more let sin and sor - row grow, Nor thorns in- fest the ground; He
4. He rules the world with truth and grace, And makes the nations prove The

ev - 'ry heart pre - pare him room, And heav'n and na-ture sing, And
fields and floods, rocks, hills and plains, Re-peat the sounding joy, Re-
comes to make his bless-ings flow Far as the curse is found, Far
glo - ries of his right-eous-ness, And wonders of his love, And

. heav'n and na-ture sing, And heav'n, And heav'n and na-ture sing.
peat the sound-ing joy, Re - peat, Re - peat the sounding joy.
as the curse is found, Far as, Far as the curse is found.
won-ders of his love, And won, And won- ders of his love.

No. 78.   I Love Thy Kingdom, Lord.

TIMOTHY DWIGHT.   HANDEL.

1. I love thy king - dom, Lord, The house of thine a - bode,
2. I love thy Church, O God! Her walls be - fore thee stand,
3. For her my tears shall fall, For her my pray'rs as - cend;
4. Be - yond my high - est joy, I prize her heav'n - ly ways,

The Church our blest Re-deem - er saved With his own pre-cious blood.
Dear as the ap - ple of thine eye, And grav - en on thy hand.
To her my cares and toils be giv'n, Till toils and cares shall end.
Her sweet com-mun - ion, sol - emn vows, Her hymns of love and praise.

No. 79. O Could I Speak the Matchless Worth.

SAMUEL MEDLEY.   Arr. by LOWELL MASON.

1. O could I speak the matchless worth, O could I sound the glo-ries forth,
2. I'd sing the precious blood he spilt, My ransom from the dreadful guilt
3. Well, the de-light-ful day will come When my dear Lord will bring me home,

Which in my Sav-ior shine, I'd soar and touch the heav'nly strings, And vie with
Of sin and wrath divine; I'd sing his glorious righteousness, In which all·
And I shall see his face; Then with my Savior, Brother, Friend, A blest e-

Ga-briel while he sings In notes almost divine, In notes almost di-vine.
per-fect, heav'nly dress My soul shall ev-er shine, My soul shall ev-er shine.
ter-ni-ty I'll spend, Triumphant in his grace, Triumphant in his grace.

No. 80.   Blest be the Tie.

JOHN FAWCETT.   HANS GEORG NAGELI.

1. Blest be   the tie   that binds Our hearts in Chris-tian love; The
2. Be-fore   our Fa-ther's throne, We pour   our   ar-dent pray'rs; Our
3. We share   our mu-tual woes,   Our mu-tual bur-dens bear; And
4. When we   a-sun-der part, It gives   us   in-ward pain; But

fel-low-ship of kin-dred minds Is   like to that a-bove.
fears, our hopes, our aims are one, Our com-forts and our cares.
oft-en for each oth-er flows The sym-pa-thiz-ing tear.
we shall still be joined in heart, And hope to meet a-gain.

64

No. 81. Awake, my Soul.

S. MEDLEY.   WESTERN MELODY.

1. A-wake, my soul, in joy-ful lays, And sing thy great Redeemer's praise;
2. He saw me ru-ined by the fall, Yet loved me, not-with-stand-ing all;
3. Tho' mighty hosts of cru-el foes, Tho' earth and hell my way op-pose,

He just-ly claims a song from me; His lov-ing kind-ness, oh, how free!
He saved me from my lost es-tate: His lov-ing kind-ness, oh, how great!
He safe-ly leads my soul a-long; His lov-ing kind-ness, oh, how strong!

His lov-ing kindness, lov-ing kindness; His loving kindness, oh, how free!
His lov-ing kindness, lov-ing kindness; His loving kindness, oh, how great!
His lov-ing kindness, lov-ing kindness; His loving kindness, oh, how strong!

No. 82. Come, Thou Fount.

R. ROBINSON.   UNKNOWN.

Fine.

1. { Come, thou Fount of ev-'ry bless-ing, Tune my heart to sing thy grace; }
   { Streams of mer-cy, nev-er ceas-ing, Call for songs of loud-est praise. }
D. C. Praise the mount—I'm fixed up-on it—Mount of thy re-deem-ing love.

2. { Here I'll raise mine Eb-en-e-zer; Hith-er by thy help I'm come; }
   { And I hope, by thy good pleasure, Safe-ly to ar-rive at home. }
D. C. He, to res-cue me from dan-ger, In-ter-posed his precious blood.

D. C.

Teach me some me-lo-dious son-net, Sung by flam-ing tongues a-bove.
Je-sus sought me when a stranger, Wand'ring from the fold of God;

E   65

No. 83.   Revive us Again.

WM. P. MACKAY.   J. J. HUSBAND.

1. We praise thee, O God! for the Son of thy love, For Jesus who
2. We praise thee, O God! for thy Spirit of light, Who has shown us our
3. All glory and praise to the Lamb that was slain, Who has borne all our
4. Revive us again; fill each heart with thy love; May each soul be re-

died and is now gone above.
Savior and scattered our night.   Hal-le-lu-jah! thine the
sins, and has cleansed ev-'ry stain.
kindled with fire from above.

glory; Hal-le-lu-jah! a-men!   Revive us again.

No. 84.   Guide me, Great Jehovah.

WILLIAM WILLIAMS.   DR. T. HASTINGS.

1. { Guide me, O thou great Je-ho-vah, Pilgrim thro' this bar-ren land: } Bread of
   { I am weak, but thou art mighty; Hold me with thy powerful hand: }
2. { O-pen now the crys-tal fountain, Whence the healing wa-ters flow; } Strong De-
   { Let the fi-ery, cloud-y pil-lar, Lead me all my journey thro': }
3. { When I tread the verge of Jordan, Bid my anxious fears subside; } Songs of
   { Bear me thro' the swelling current; Land me safe on Canaan's side: }

heaven, Feed me till I want no more. Bread of heaven, Feed me till I want no more.
liverer, Be thou still my strength and shield. Strong Deliverer, Be thou still my strength and shield.
praises I will ev-er give to thee. Songs of praises I will ev-er give to thee.

No. 85. How Firm a Foundation.

GEORGE KEITH.   UNKNOWN.

1. How firm a foun-da-tion, ye saints of the Lord, Is laid for your
2. Fear not, I am with thee, O be not dismayed, For I am thy
3. When through the deep wa-ters I call thee to go, The riv-ers of
4. When through fier-y tri-als thy pathway shall lie, My grace, all-suf-

faith in his ex-cel-lent word! What more can he say, than to
God, I will still give thee aid; I'll strengthen thee, help thee, and
sor-row shall not o-ver-flow; For I will be with thee thy
fi-cient, shall be thy sup-ply, The flame shall not hurt thee; I

you he hath said, To you, who for ref-uge to Je-sus have
cause thee to stand, Up-held by my gracious, om-nip-o-tent
tri-als to bless, And sanc-ti-fy to thee thy deep-est dis-
on-ly de-sign Thy dross to consume, and thy gold to re-

fied? To you, who for ref-uge to Je-sus have fled?
hand, Up-held by my gra-cious, om-nip-o-tent hand.
tress, And sanc-ti-fy to thee thy deep-est dis-tress.
fine, Thy dross to con-sume, and thy gold to re-fine.

5 E'en down to old age all my people
    shall prove
My sovereign, eternal, unchangeable love;
And when hoary hairs shall their temples adorn,
Like lambs they shall still in my bosom
    be borne.

6 The soul that on Jesus hath leaned
    for repose,
I will not, I will not desert to his foes;
That soul, though all hell should en-
    deavor to shake,
I'll never, no never, no never forsake!

67

No. 86. **Forever Here my Rest.**

CHARLES WESLEY.   HUGH WILSON.

1. For - ev - er here my rest shall be, Close to thy bleed-ing side;
2. My dy - ing Sav - ior and my God, Fountain for guilt and sin,
3. Wash me, and make me thus thine own ; Wash me, and mine thou art;
4. Th' a-tonement of thy blood ap - ply, Till faith to sight im - prove;

This all my hope, and all my plea, "For me the Sav - ior died."
Sprin-kle me ev - er with thy blood, And cleanse and keep me clean.
Wash me, but not my feet a - lone, My hands, my head, my heart.
Till hope in full fru - i - tion die, And all my soul be love.

No. 87. O, for a Heart to Praise.

1 O for a heart to praise my God,
  A heart from sin set free!
A heart that always feels thy blood,
  So freely spilt for me!

2 A heart resigned, submissive, meek,
  My great Redeemer's throne;
Where only Christ is heard to speak,
  Where Jesus reigns alone.

3 O for a lowly, contrite heart,
  Believing, true, and clean,
Which neither life nor death can part
  From Him that dwells within!

4 A heart in every thought renewed,
  And full of love divine;
Perfect, and right, and pure, and good,
  A copy, Lord, of thine.

No. 88. Come, Humble Sinner.

1 Come, humble sinner, in whose breast
  A thousand thoughts revolve,
Come, with your guilt and fear oppressed,
  And make this last resolve :—

2 I 'll go to Jesus, though my sin
  Like mountains round me close;
I know his courts, I 'll enter in,
  Whatever may oppose.

3 Perhaps he will admit my plea,
  Perhaps will hear my prayer ;
But, if I perish, I will pray,
  And perish only there.

4 I can but perish if I go ;
  I am resolved to try ;
For if I stay away, I know
  I must forever die.

EDMUND JONES.

No. 89. Jesus, Great Shepherd.

1 Jesus, great Shepherd of the sheep,
  To thee for help we fly;
Thy little flock in safety keep,
  For O, the wolf is nigh !

2 He comes, of hellish malice full,
  To scatter, tear, and slay;
He seizes every straggling soul
  As his own lawful prey.

3 Us into thy protection take
  And gather with thine arm ;
Unless the fold we first forsake,
  The wolf can never harm.

4 Together let us sweetly live,
  Together let us die;
And each a starry crown receive,
  And reign above the sky.

CHARLES WESLEY.

68

No. 90. Walk in the Light.

B. BARTON.   FROM MEHUL AND HAYDN.

1. Walk in the light! so shalt thou know That fel-low-ship of love,
2. Walk in the light! and thou shalt find Thy heart made tru-ly his,
3. Walk in the light! and thou shalt own Thy darkness passed a-way,
4. Walk in the light! thy path shall be Peace-ful, serene, and bright:

His Spir - it on - ly can be- stow Who reigns in light a - bove.
Who dwells in cloudless light enshrined, In whom no darkness is.
Be - cause that light hath on thee shone In which is per - fect day.
For God, by grace, shall dwell in thee, And God himself is light.

No. 91. O What Amazing Words.

1 O what amazing words of grace
   Are in the gospel found!
Suited to every sinner's case,
   Who knows the joyful sound.

2 Poor, sinful, thirsty, fainting souls
   Are freely welcome here ;
Salvation, like a river, rolls
   Abundant, free, and clear.

3 Come, then, with all your wants and wounds;
   Your every burden bring :
Here love, unchanging love, abounds,
   A deep, celestial spring.

4 Millions of sinners, vile as you,
   Have here found life and peace ;
Come, then, and prove its virtues too,
   And drink, adore, and bless.
                                    S. MEDLEY.

No. 92. Return, O Wanderer.

1 Return, O wanderer, return,
   And seek thy Father's face ;
Those new desires which in thee burn
   Were kindled by his grace.

2 Return, O wanderer, return ;
   He hears thy humble sigh :
He sees thy softened spirit mourn,
   When no one else is nigh.

3 Return, O wanderer, return ;
   Thy Savior bids thee live :
Come to his cross, and, grateful, learn
   How freely he 'll forgive.

4 Return, O wanderer, return,
   And wipe the falling tear ;
Thy Father calls,—no longer mourn ;
   'T is love invites thee near.
                                    W. B. COLLYER.

No. 93. Victorious Love.

1 Jesus, thine all-victorious love
   Shed in my heart abroad :
Then shall my feet no longer rove,
   Rooted and fixed in God.

2 O that in me the sacred fire
   Might now begin to glow,
Burn up the dross of base desire
   And make the mountains flow !

3 O that it now from heaven might fall,
   And all my sins consume !
Come, Holy Ghost, for thee I call ;
   Spirit of burning, come !

4 Refining fire, go through my heart ;
   Illuminate my soul ;
Scatter thy life through every part,
   And sanctify the whole.
                                    C. WESLEY.

No. 94. Of Him who did Salvation Bring.

BERNARD OF CLAIRVAUX. Tr. by BOEHM. LOWELL MASON.

1. Of Him who did sal - va - tion bring, I could for - ev - er think and sing;
2. Ask but his grace, and lo, 'tis given; Ask, and he turns your hell to heaven;
3. To shame our sins he blushed in blood; He closed his eyes to show us God:
4. In - sa - tiate to this spring I fly; I drink, and yet am ev - er dry:

A - rise, ye need - y,—he'll re-lieve; A -rise, ye guilt- y,—he'll forgive.
Though sin and sor-row wound my soul, Je - sus, thy balm will make it whole.
Let all the world fall down and know That none but God such love can show.
Ah! who against thy charms is proof? Ah! who that loves, can love enough?

No. 95. The Gift Unspeakable.

1 Happy the man who finds the grace,
The blessing of God's chosen race,
The wisdom coming from above,
The faith that sweetly works by love.

2 Wisdom divine! who tells the price
Of wisdom's costly merchandise?
Wisdom to silver we prefer,
And gold is dross compared to her.

3 Her hands are filled with length of days,
True riches, and immortal praise;
Her ways are ways of pleasantness,
And all her flowery paths are peace.

4 Happy the man who wisdom gains;
Thrice happy, who his guest retains:
He owns, and shall forever own,
Wisdom, and Christ, and heaven are one.
CHARLES WESLEY.

No. 96. The Gospel Feast.

1 Come, sinners, to the gospel feast;
Let every soul be Jesus' guest;
Ye need not one be left behind,
For God hath bidden all mankind.

2 Sent by my Lord, on you I call;
The invitation is to all;
Come all the world! come, sinner thou!
All things in Christ are ready now.

3 Come, all ye souls by sin oppressed,
Ye restless wanderers after rest;
Ye poor, and maimed, and halt, and blind,
In Christ a hearty welcome find.

4 My message as from God receive;
Ye all may come to Christ and live;
O let his love your hearts constrain,
Nor suffer him to die in vain.
C. WESLEY.

No. 97. Entirely Thine.

1 Lord, I am thine, entirely thine,
Purchased and saved by blood divine;
With full consent thine I would be,
And own thy sovereign right in me.

2 Grant one poor sinner more a place
Among the children of thy grace;
A wretched sinner, lost to God,
But ransomd by Immanuel's blood.

3 Thine would I live, thine would I die,
Be thine through all eternity;
The vow is past beyond repeal,
And now I set the solemn seal.

4 Here, at that cross where flows the blood
That bought my guilty soul for God,
Thee, my new Master, now I call,
And consecrate to thee my all.
SAMUEL DAVIES.

No. 98.　　　Old Hundred,

Praise God, from whom all bless-ings flow; Praise him, all creatures here be - low;

Praise him a - bove, ye heav'nly host; Praise Father, Son, and Ho - ly Ghost.

No. 99.　　　Sessions.

Praise God, from whom all blessings flow; Praise him, all creatures here below;

Praise him a-bove, ye heav'nly host; Praise Father, Son, and Ho-ly Ghost.

No. 100.　Thirsting for Perfect Love.

1 I thirst, thou wounded Lamb of God,
To wash me in thy cleansing blood;
To dwell within thy wounds; then pain
Is sweet, and life or death is gain.

2 Take my poor heart, and let it be
Forever closed to all but thee:
Seal thou my breast, and let me wear
That pledge of love forever there.

3 How blest are they who still abide
Close sheltered in thy bleeding side!
Who thence their life and strength derive,
And by thee move, and in thee live.

4. Hence our hearts melt, our eyes o'erflow,
Our words are lost, nor will we know,
Nor will we think of aught beside,
"My Lord, my Love is crucified."

NICOLAUS L. ZINZENDORF. Tr. by J. WESLEY.

INDEX.

www.ingramcontent.com/pod-product-compliance
Lightning Source LLC
Chambersburg PA
CBHW021528270326
41930CB00008B/1152

*9 7 8 3 3 3 7 2 6 6 1 7 2 *